no dogs in heaven
by Scott Mason

Cleveland State University Poetry Center

Cleveland Poets Series No. 24

The author would like to acknowledge the following publications, in which some of these poems first appeared:
The Cleveland Anthology: "something more you should know"
The Dovetail Joint: "white haze"
Gegenschein Quarterly: "second degree"
The Green Horse for Poetry: "an i'm the one"
Itinerary and *Song:* "amplitude"

Front cover photo by Scott Mason

Publication of this book was made possible through a grant from the Ohio Arts Council, which is hereby gratefully acknowledged.

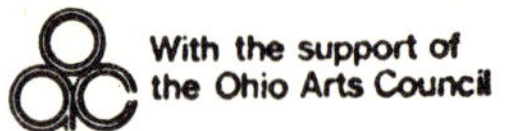

table of contents

I am playing with my own cards.
I have loaded the dice.
I have drugged that little horse called Death.
— Kenneth Patchen
from *The Journal of Albion Moonlight*

For Therese

an i'm the one

what we were
was kids
was bad & was dirty
& mouthy

and there is plenty
cause for these effects
why we honk honk
our lavender horns
and drive our studded bodies
on the elders' lackluster lawns

the traveler

& it gets dark early
                like a warning
rain's soft display
cushion's the blow

                    plain smoke
                    & simple

        mr K. W.   walkin

got my foot in it   i remember
i was running   out
over the red glow of a city   here   or   there
out   an   alone
                    my spirit juggling in the
dark side mirrors
                    roadie and the zoo keeper
                    come nosin my back door
runnin about a mile behind
kickin ass on my twin axle 13 speed ranger
5,6,7,8,   wingin my arm around andy devine
                9,10...
                            goddam buckaroos
            we're goin into the big canyon   11,12

2.
we lived in townie town
went over everynite to pigtown

felt nice

right at home   black velvet

up and down the rail   we liked to puditon our hair &

red & vestal grabbed lonnie (a mexican ice boy)
caught him messin with their snowmobile
ought call the game warden sd red
buttfuckya rite here sd vestal

us bluelites went to travelin up to the sheraton
clean facilities
went to parties in rented rooms
slide shows
wore our animal dyed skins & hides
                rinnie wore her pointed lizard faced shoes
we made some hits
me & slick & the boys from gastown
till the highway crew showed
and got on us in their loaded pickem up trucks
sat on us and they tried burning out our toes

the blizzard over
i threw my log book onto the fire
walked out to my rig (tiger lily) parked right outside
        hit the cushions
                blew off some steam
                        brought up pressure

slipped er into greasy
chugged back out on & up
kipton nickle plate Hwy
looked over in the sleeper   4,5...
LONNIE!! 6,7,
how's yr ass boy!
just fine capt'n 10,11,12,

        13!

from the alligator notebooks

alligators will kill you
alligators will eat your kid
alligators can run faster than a dog
alligators can make great shoes
they can smile & me or you would shoot them
for no good reason

alligators have four eyelids
you can hold an alligator's mouth shut & wrestle with him
but usually they attack with surprise &
blitzkrieg your calf or thigh
at night though
alligators do get sad
& go home late at night
empty   alone
downright   outtaluck

someone by herself

take a woman & we'll call her sky
she'll belong in the sun
it will fill over the pores in the face
backlight the hair & bodice
silhouette her against the green sea

we think it is all to our supreme good fortune
but she is more than the eyes in our hands
let me tell you how free she is
lookit here
she know nothing but true stories
about the foreskin and the whippoorwill it's jus
we know there will soon be something heavy around her
look here   there she is in the street   in the city
placing the thinnest cigarette toward her lips
picking still another means of attack or defense
she burns on   on
the sheer nails of nerve ends

maybe the lights in the dark would scare her
and she would be excitable   like children before the storm
soon she will be given little credit
becoming a part of our present   and then   glimpse in the past

American Locomotive Co.

my dad worked for alco
& we used to go to the plant
past the watchmen winding clocks
dick or neil or abe
gave me a badge
and the old brick plant
had dark green doors
small plots of grass
& red yard hydrants
we used to sneak in mr. elvin's office
sit in his chair & look through his trash
my dad up there welding
sparks winging out around his head
whole place going up in smoke
my dad's welding shield on the back seat car shelf
and after work
spin over to shep's
shep's tooth pick & cigarette
& shep's cap   feels himself
in his pocket pool parlor
watching those horses pull at their beer
then we went out
stand down on the state route
& i saw ace doran
hair raised up on the back of my neck
at midnight
his blue gunmetal 55 reo
his fine superchargers wound up & whistling
burning on the clean night air

plan for the future

for mario

i'm saying to you now on the ground as the night closes over us hands & feet telling the body to sleep
"fathers of our doctrines we'd never be like you
a thing like trouble points at our hearts
we came right from the womb speaking secret & hidden things   shaking from the very start
there must be something wrong with us

listen now under the poplar trees clapping
you are entering doldrums
it is foggy & the dampness settling   going through the motions   so much likened to so many things
and still so unafraid   your slicked back hair greased hands & bungled face
all of a sudden you saw your poor concrete   the job in the used water factory
each day how it led us forward yet further away
you saw the world as real as blood on white feathers   everything   what'd it been put here for
look now   your arm shooting out to strike at somethingone
o god now imagine   nothing completely attached

think it through   wind rushing over you
the time as it was ment for us   nonsense   like the calender girl & the day coming up on the other side
of the world   inca black night opening to reveal the stars
they point the direction & have voices lighting your journey   arcing through the air
suddenly you're the only one
under the stars tonight

antfarm

clover growing & laid out sweet for square mile
for the cows   velvet dogs
                smells sweet as gasoline in the old "Chambers"
clumps of compost spattering every man woman child
lookout! we had to put some bull chips in for shingles
& cornfritters for satisfaction!
skunk cabbage auntie boiled up
we eat the fetid earth in mid-continent
(like gloucester sucks its oysters raw)
i went up into the greenhills rolling for miles
licked my lips as fat as butter
hoed another row   caterpillars in my hair
                and those big velvet dogs
                cake walked
                over the last leg home
                their slaughtered eyes straight ahead

sun a little lower veiled through grey clouds
we cover our mouths   FALL! perhaps september
trees rustle & shift to the other leg
night bitters   snapping the citrus in the twat

sun glistens off our black exoskeleton
stooped & crossing a ridge
snow begins punching us in the face
gaze down between cracks in the timbered loft
hear the pigs sloshing far below in the hold
steaming animals milling around
snow sifting over our mouths at night

winter   don't forget

*

out comes the sun   just that simply
we see how dirty everything has gotten by some miracle of neglect
something dying in the walls
women pickup shovels to offset the entire year
somehow their voices seem to hold up their bodies
echo through the streets & neighborhoods
if only i could take something from the sky and give it to them

**

women and men following thin waves of their minds like
                                        complete strangers
bunching up in crowds   they have masks & police masters
                                        heads in windows
with lights behind   rooms smelling of sleep   one time streets
and wet lips kneading the air   warming the afternoons
all the questions marking the minds
unchanging as the scars on the face and hands

***

i ride the train with the people from the city of snow
people of guns & plastic shoes
where do they live?
i know
grey natural & the beautiful stench
a civilization of men with giant structures and short hair
if only i could tell them of the warmth of seasons
          city clouded in thing called air
that all around them lies corn fallowed beneath snow

amplitude

in between
the heavily conceived
trills and vibrato
of an electric blues
guitar solo
we hear a barking dog
      what he say
      what he say is
      i love my sweet
      baby
what he say is
don't hold your breath
but fetch another witness
what he say
is pro-men-ade
promenade

discord i

at once
up pops our fresh face
brash & amused as aluminum foil

how should we be taken?
as a clown? an arse?
what's this smudged
all over fresh face?

a trifle misguided
we are here
to nozzle & mew
'gainst our loved ones
but at once
we draw back from faces
as they turn white & purple
neonic   in sleep

discord ii

at once
we go out and start the car
go back inside
get into bed
with our loved ones
only to be returning later
to find the water
hot
only to be returning
to find our loved ones   departed
to find the car   gone
and the note
            you have bummed us out
            this friday
            yr not such a good time

discord iii

at once
ashes fall down around us
like the floors in a building collapse
desks & pencil sets cascading to the same ground
where are there rooms
for the ghosts of small childhood animals
in the wee hrs
ghosts of cigarette butts come to stand in our drawers
and their ashes
are falling down
around us

in the wee hrs
we make a cut & paste job of it
falling through the branches
of dead trees   like the floors of old buildings
our bodies are fragile
in the upper atmosphere
we are falling down
around ourselves
in the wee hrs
falling asleep
in the poem

the hokey pokey

we was like this
all twisted up with crackers comin outta our mouths
and she   she was like this   and loose
just poppin outta her body
wouldn't listen when they
won't her
she'd always say how you all do tonight
down at the Eldorado
                    rocking to that box of lights
she'd never have any money
always stayed awhile somehow
said she didn't need no money
she was free somehow
like about a 1000 great hand jobs
she said she was of Southern California
                              she said   baby
                    we gotta go   slow
              i think of her every chance i can

the jimi hendrix experience

i thought the guitar said blitzkrieg blitzkrieg
go out and bomb it down
but what it said was fingers & toes fingers & toes
ride me into the sky

jimi wrote a song and said it was a poem
& i followed him all over the world
finding out what a guitar could do

his lips three spaces behind my ear
"nobody know what i'm talkin about"
heh

he was burning down
he was so close to where he was going
"not to die but to be reborn
away from a land so battered and torn"

i thought 600 miles per hr
skimming over the waves
but he was right here   one before
& one after

no dogs in heaven

out slinks the sheriff's deputy
his face growing in the street light
he is out to see the "sisters" performing
the fab stewardesses cloning
he punches his sniper face right through the rain
he's hot boy
he's hot on the pistolas of the urban fringe
wallowing around in the mud streets
he's dripping with mud
what's this?
he finds a small body under the mud
black and wilted as an ingrown hair
his carbuncles are acting up
he pockets the teabag body
the rain starts up
& the rain stops
everything dries up
and mud cracks on his face
dust puffts from his clothes
he trips over a hand   too bad louse
he thinks   tick farmer   lizard lips
(the arm of the law...   he thinks
                         the arm of the law...   )
he reaches the office   there's some red
tranny fluid on the floor
("shit" he says under his breath)
there's a half rebuilt rear end in the corner
"the arm of the law is criminal silence" he says
his boils swell a bit
he too quickly gets up and looks out the window
loses his balance   he reaches for his piece
he hears the sound of his 44
he crumples down onto the mud caked floor

he blacks out in a history of Jonestown

crossfade

station wagon
coke can with straw in hand attached
Lee stumbles into a child
swerves & puts the pedal to metal   grips tighter his mauser
pigeons disintegrate

Betty blew her hair dry
clasped her purse   Ooo let's go for some dinner
she puts her hand in his & go out the front
Jack Ruby walks around the corner   Hi Jack, Betty says
Jack has a big round smile   Hi Betty!
he meets Fedora in the alley
custodian of his child   on a leash & as sensible
as his revving & rammy how much you sell way with the world
even now he feels threatened
of being blown   Kaboom!   off the face of the map
not to mention Checkers his wife
she points up   the sky comes out but
only illuminating the grey stoned asphalt of his shingles
see   she says   that's where daddy works

Jack crumples his faded suit & stuffs it in behind
steps in for a couple quick heaters
his small pudgy legs moving unbelievably in the Texas heat
he runs down the jazzbo as he goes
the crowd makes heat
chumps like a flock of horseflies
big black limos line the curbs
he's on to the culprit now

Texarkana

lonerider
panhead   whiskey for fuel
he thought he'd go out and breed
the farm and the locusts and the bullshittin hogs
worked his way south
he never thought about jail
or thought they'd slam him around   a blumberin'
lucky he carried a sidearm
                        Crystal asked him not to
but he got into it with a house detective
over some old six bit acey deucy
& shot a man in Pecos

Buzz Aldren looked through the firewall at the moon's surface
he rotated his giant galvanized capsule
                        they had affectioned   "Nite Train"
he conjures an image of Toots & Evie
he wonders if they got the bucking bull rodeo underway by now

just standin around
no bronc bustin in sight
got drunk down around Juarez
got his fist around that town's throat
that was all she wrote
put to some hard travelin
a posse in border town got on his dim trail
he led em back around
rode right over that town like a mudslide

"Buzz ?" Neil says
Buzz drifts back to his breeding days
thinks of his prize Louella
the lights of the control panel shade from yellow to orange to red
the capsule nears the final approach
he grabs the retro throttles from underneath
sidles it down
then he puts it over hard and nails it a couple a times
the blinding light reflects off his visor
the TV cameras switch on
the gate opens & the crowd goes kablooey

second degree

I
and the randomness
of violence, Sheerness,
the thin skin you get
to escape in.
the chrome in violence,
more than in death.

you get a gun
words move like knives
but will not bury into the face

you go to his front door
and blast him
full in the face
and you don't care
about how dead is dead
black piano keys fill your head

later
they splice & orchestrate
and you can remember and remember
in white light
remember through concrete and mattress
& . . .
but not in the context
of twelve silent faces
not in so many calm words

II
and the cops
in their midnight & chrome,
and all those they beat,
their faces, their balls,
how they beat them goddam good and blue.

they came up behind and i sd "shit steve they want us" we
pulled over   i saw the one had a pistol on steve and the
other had a shotgun on me   not balancing it in his one
hand   lolling the heft between his fingers but both hands
firm on barrel & stock   rigid stance   they search us and
the car   one went back to the car with the flasher on but the
one with the shotgun stayed   traffic slowed   "goddam em"
steve sd and i kept looking down the open black holes saying
this is a real gun gun gun   scratched blue sheened
barrel   scratched dirty silver underneath   i could feel the
coldness of the barrel   even in the heat   could feel an ex-
plosion furrow deep in my pulpy face   my teeth powder my
chest a dream of red bones   and how i'd go down   hunch
of falling   faint click of preconception   prickly heat of an-
ticipation   click   narrow knuckle punch of ham-
mer   click   and a race between smooth turned surfaces
and reflexes   neuron-synapse-neuron-synapse race through
fibrils 220mph

    the cars   they'd slow way down

one two they smash you down
you float behind momentum
and once down
they're doing their worst to
yr face & balls
all yr blood like warm oil
smell of it all in yr nose
hopeless hopeless
crack of yr knuckles & bones
up against blue steel and chrome
the numbness of a deep nerve in the
face or pain so deep there is
the feel of air on bone

white haze

wouldn't close the windows
      nonono no

"oh he'll never stop never stop"
      nono no

i was like a star in their not-too-much lives

oh he'll never stop
finding pictures in the rain

the servants all gone in the night
i wouldn't close the windows
      on&on&on

wouldn't close
no the windows

so close
& so dark
like blank channels

the summer ends

new street wise crowd just out
sporty new wide cuff pants
new high waisted flannel rice paper pants
shoes of yellow or brown
with flannel repeat tweed inserts
last linen flames of August virus in the air
the swingos lite up then pat down & wipe off their machines
re-dos of skiffle songs tinning out of their rear windows
they get out the barbells and in time
apply themselves like jobs

two new suits with ties let out
they wade into the newstands waving their tweed arms
like an attitude they've got about cordovan
the street crowd follows in behind yelling
Hey Angel! Hey Kid Cool! Hey Stuff!
light filters down between high clouds
a cool wind lifts
the crowd parts and the headline jumps out
WHERE SUMMER ENDS and underneath
as though a stuttered afterthought
"where one time the soft spread out like a hum job"

something more you should know

i was thinking about a life & spirit ruinated
but giving light where portions had been shot away and
cleansed

maybe you are selling dolls or giving tours
or opening clams or sitting back letting everyday
hit you as hard as it can   or are you just at a stopping off point
or are you actually settled into habit
nudging beans up an incline with a rough stick

maybe you move graves or drive big steamer trunks
on the highways   your fathers would be quick to tell you
the tigers of wrath are wiser than the horses of instruction
those before found it acceptable to get in on the groundfloor
hookup and coast along putting miles on those behind them
to be lazy like trees with most of their lives always past

i was sitting sucking hot embers into my throat
and collecting enough memories to move on with the next storm cent
push through the swamps on the south end of the island
get to the shore
and write my name in huge letters in the sand